Table of Contents

Kit Connor is best known for playing Nick Nelson in *Heartstopper*.

Meet Kit Connor

Kit Connor is a British actor. He has been on TV and in movies. Connor starred in the Netflix TV series *Heartstopper*. He has acted in plays, too. This young man is talented in many ways.

Growing Up

Connor was born in Croydon, England. He was very shy when he was little. His parents sent him to an acting class to help him. Connor loved acting. Soon, he was **auditioning** for TV shows and movies.

Connor started acting as a child and quickly became popular.

Connor attended the premiere of *Get Santa* in 2014.

Get Santa

Connor made his **debut** when he was nine years old. He played small parts in different TV shows. Then, in 2014, he was in a movie. It was called *Get Santa*. Connor's character helped save Christmas. **Critics** liked Connor. They said he acted very well.

EARLY WORK

Connor also had small parts in the movies *Mr. Holmes* (2015) and *Ready Player One* (2018).

Connor (left) appears with his costars from *The Mercy* (2018).

Making Movies

After the success of *Get Santa*, Connor got other movie **roles**. In 2018, he had a small part in the movie *The Mercy*. He played the son of the main character. This part helped him get ready for bigger roles in the future.

Young Rocket

In 2019, Connor was in the movie *Rocketman*. He played a young version of rock star Elton John. Connor had a lot of fun making the movie. He loved meeting Elton John!

MUSIC LESSONS
Connor learned to play piano and sing for *Rocketman*.

In *Rocketman* (2019), Connor played young Elton John, who was called Reggie as a child.

Connor starred in *Heartstopper* with Joe Locke.

Heartstopper

In 2022, a new show came on the streaming service Netflix. It was called *Heartstopper*. The show is about two teenage boys who fall in love. Connor played Nick Nelson. Fans loved the show. Connor helped people feel more comfortable about their **sexuality**.

DID YOU KNOW?
Nick Nelson is a rugby player. Connor lifted weights and worked out for the role.

Award Winner

Connor has won awards for his work. In 2023, he won a Children's and Family Emmy for *Heartstopper*. He played a kind and brave character. He has been **nominated** for other awards, too. Many people say he is a very talented actor.

HELPING OTHERS

Connor has raised money to help people with medical needs. He has also raised money for the Animal League.

In 2022, Connor and
Joe Locke were named
GQ Men of the Year.

Voice Actor

Connor played other roles, as well. He played the voice of Pan in the BBC TV series *His Dark Materials* (2019–2022). Pan takes the shape of many different animals. Connor also voiced Brightbill in the movie *The Wild Robot* (2024).

In 2024, Connor voiced a goose in the DreamWorks movie *The Wild Robot*.

Connor played Romeo in *Romeo + Juliet* from October 2024 until February 2025.

Broadway and Beyond

In 2024, Connor made the move to Broadway theater. He starred as Romeo in *Romeo + Juliet*. The show was very popular. Connor is still making movies, too. There's no telling what this actor will do next!

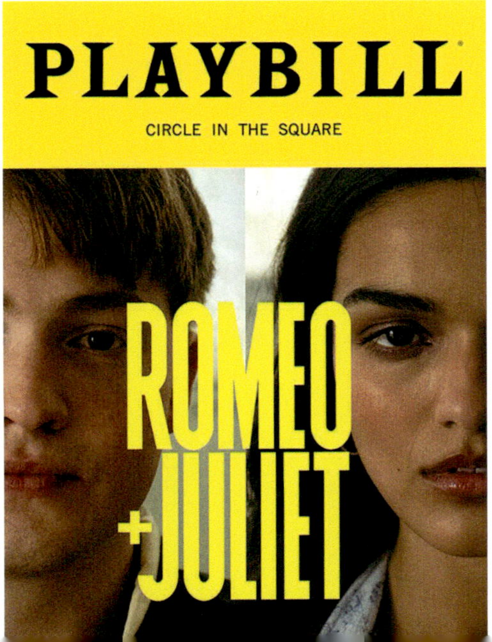

SUPER STATS

KIT SEBASTIAN CONNOR

Birthday: March 8, 2004

Birthplace: Croydon, England

TV Roles: *Heartstopper* (2022–2024), *His Dark Materials* (voice, 2019–2022), *Rocket's Island* (2014–2015)

Film Roles: *Warfare* (2025), *The Wild Robot* (voice, 2024), *Rocketman* (2019), *Get Santa* (2014)

Professional Theater: *Romeo + Juliet* (2024–2025)

AWARDS

Queerty Awards: 2024

Royal Television Society Programme Winner: 2024

Children's and Family Emmy Award: 2023

GQ Men of the Year Award: 2022

GLOSSARY

audition A tryout for a performing part.

critic A person who says what they like and don't like about a performance.

debut A person's first time performing.

nominate To choose as a candidate for office or an award.

role A part played by an actor.

sexuality A person's self-identification as bisexual, straight, gay, pansexual, etc.

READ MORE

Bisantz, Max. **What Is the Story of Romeo and Juliet?** Penguin Workshop, 2023.

Grack, Rachel. **Curious About Netflix.** Amicus Learning, 2026.

ON THE WEB

IMDb: Kit Connor
https://www.imdb.com/name/nm5598573/

Kiddle: Kit Connor facts for kids
https://kids.kiddle.co/Kit_Connor

INDEX

About the Author

Joanne Mattern is the author of hundreds of nonfiction books for children. Her favorite subjects are biographies, sports, animals, and history. Joanne loves learning new things and sharing that knowledge with young readers! She lives in New York State with her family.